Da

Walk With Confidence

The Path is Already Cleared

Dale Leighton Campbell

Copyright © 2022 Dale Leighton Campbell
All Rights Reserved
ISBN: 9798806195853

Dale Leighton Campbell

No part of this book may be used or reproduced in any matter, without written consent, except in the case of reprints in the context of reviews.

Email:
daleleightonpatrickcampbell@gmail.com

Published by Unfiltered Pages Publishing House.

Dale Leighton Campbell

Introduction

This is a collection of poems written over a period of time. They are inspired by the Lord, and they span multiple topics that we face throughout this lifetime. It is my hope that you will enjoy these poems and find the lesson in each of them.

God teaches us in different ways, and it is important that we are open to receiving those teachings. These poems are reflections of some of the lessons that I have learnt throughout my life thus far.

Dale Leighton Campbell

Acknowledgements

I first want to express my gratitude to God for placing this gift inside of me and allowing me to share these thoughts with the rest of the world.

I'd also like to thank the Blackstocks, the Mills, the Gowies, and the Johnsons for their support. Finally, Minister Gordon, she told me to get these poems published, without knowing how; this would not have happened without her. Thank you.

Dale Leighton Campbell

Table of Contents

Introduction 3

Acknowledgements 4

God is Everything Everywhere 6

When God is Ready, Will You Be? 9

How Firm Are Your Feet? 11

Are You Sure Who You Are? 13

There is Hope for Everyone 15

Be Confident in God 17

Make Sure Our Place is Secure 19

Who is Our Father? 21

The Nature of the Seasons 24

Will You Do What I Say? 27

Keep At It, Don't Stop 29

For Someone Special 31

Open The Gift That You Got 34

Don't Let It Get To The Grave 38

Restoration. Healing. Unity 41

Notes 43

About the Author 47

Dale Leighton Campbell

God Is Everything Everywhere

When we need an answer from God, we go to him in earnest supplication
We serve God and keep all his commandments, so that there is no condemnation.
Then we must prepare ourselves in all our ways to make the right accommodation
And wherever the word of God is, we must be in active participation.

Walking uprightly in God, keeping his statutes, this is our reputation
To stand on the word of God and put up a demonstration
For God has called us out into holiness as one in the spirit, this is our adaptation
But still, when Satan couldn't get what he wanted, he tried to take out his frustration.

But we trust in God for power over our
enemies, for the ultimate domination
After we try to do things on our own and
we fail, this is our realization
And when we do fail, our father sets us
right again and gives us purification
I thank God for his Mercy and Love which
he gave to me in restoration.

Even then, Satan comes to God with our
souls trying to make a lot of accusations
But there is hope for us in God's word,
which is stated in the book of
Lamentations
So, let us pray to God that he fills us with
his holy ghost, this is his recommendation
And when we worship the Almighty, his
presence will come over us with a glorious
sensation.

Dale Leighton Campbell

So, we lift our heads towards Heaven, for the coming of Jesus in glorious anticipation
Following his teachings and doing his will, then will he take us to or final destination.

7.6.21

Dale Leighton Campbell

When God Is Ready, Will You Be?

The beginning of our Father in our lives is
the start of a good foundation
So, we put everything in God to do his
work, this is his administration
And we obey our God and keep his
commandments, this is our participation.

The word of God is mapped out with
instructions
There is no better illustration
Let us stay close to our Father, there
should be absolutely no separation.

Then we come together worshipping and
giving God all the glory in the
congregation
So, study the word of God in depth, and he
will give you the right interpretation

Dale Leighton Campbell

Jehovah gave us all that we have in him for our habitation.

For all things are possible with God because he gave us the authorization
And when we come together in Christ, let righteousness be in our conversation
When we fail God, we must come clean, and he will give us restoration.

So Jesus came into our lives and changed it, this is our proclamation
For the Almighty cares about us in everything, he, and he alone is our inspiration
Jesus is coming back for his people, so we must make the final preparation.

And before you enter the kingdom of God, you must have the right identification.

7.8.21

Dale Leighton Campbell

How Firm Are Your Feet?

As Jesus enters your life, your whole
pattern becomes clean and neat
Settle in the gospel of Jesus so that Satan
cannot move you from your seat.

Then we carry ourselves into holiness and
Jesus is the one we must repeat
You won't know unless you try, and then
you will find out that salvation is sweet.

Everything that we say and do,
righteousness should be in the path of our
feet
On your walk with Jesus, the devil will
attack, then you must dig in with your
cleats.

Make sure the word of God is the main
thing we eat

Because the word of the gospel is good, especially when it gets into the potatoes and the meat.

Then when we come in one accord against Satan, he has to flea because he can't take the heat
As we go down the road of life, God made Jesus available, and him, I am glad to meet.

When we go into the kingdom, all saints we will see, but Jesus will be the main one that we will greet.

7.12.21

Dale Leighton Campbell

Are You Sure Who You Are?

When Jesus shed his blood on Calvary, and
rose again, the works of Satan fell
And when we are under the influence of
Satan, it seems like we're under a spell.

But we don't want anything to do with the
devil, especially what he has to sell
Because the gospel of Jesus changes our
lives, so wherever we go, we must tell.

We should keep our bodies, the temple of
God, clean, because this is where he dwells
But if we continue in sin, being disobedient
to God is a one-way ticket to hell.

If it was up the devil all the way, he would
love to keep us in a shell

Dale Leighton Campbell

But with the power of God and the name of Jesus, when Satan is around, he has to repel.

So, when Sunday comes, we know it's time for church by the ringing of the bell
And we exercise the fruit of the spirit, starting with love which we expand and swell.

Then when the holy ghost comes over our souls, it's like a sweet perfume that we smell
And when we have assurance with God, we can sing with our souls, 'it is well'.

7.16.21

Dale Leighton Campbell

There Is Hope For Everyone

You've come to the junction point for all roads, be sure it's the right one that you pick
For the pace of our salvation is steady, try not to be too quick.

Because the word of God is clean, so let us make it stick
Don't let Satan attach himself to you, he will drain your righteousness like a tick.

Sometimes the road you're on is shaky, but God will protect you even when it gets slick
Still, there is lots of like for God, even when the enemy thinks he has us licked.

Didn't he know that there is no other closer than Jesus? He and I are thick

Dale Leighton Campbell

And when you have a relationship with
such a friend, things will start to click.

So don't let Satan burn out your lamp,
make sure there is always oil on the wick
Still the devil comes in our minds with
evil, trying to make us fall for the trick.

But in the name of Jesus, like a football,
the devil we're going to kick
Despite the kicking, he comes in all forms,
trying to make us sick.

So, wherever he is, by the blood of Jesus,
we will evict
And we stand on the foundation that God
has built, with Jesus as the main brick.

8.9.21

Dale Leighton Campbell

Be Confident In God

When there are decisions to make, be sure it is Jesus that you are choosing
And on our Christian journey, God must be the one that we are always proving.

Trials and temptations will come our way, to see if we are snoozing
So walk upright in the Lord and refrain from evil, because those things are not amusing.

Satan will try everything to shut us down, but God will stop the abusing
And when we hurt someone's feelings, we go to them with love in excusing.

For the words from the devil's mouth are a curse, but from God they are soothing

Then when we get on this highway of life,
you and Jesus will be cruising.

We know that no matter what Satan
thinks or says about us, God will not
accept the accusing
Still the enemy will test us left and right,
but to God he is looking for a bruising.

So, whatever the wicked one tries, Lord
knows he will always be losing.

12.14.21

Dale Leighton Campbell

Make Sure Our Place Is Secure

The love of Jesus is extended to everyone in the human race
And when you commit your life to him, all your sins he will erase.
So, stay steady as we go on in life, believe Jesus and he will give us the right pace
But the devil is always sneaking around, and we must never give him any space.

For Jesus is the one to look to, who will keep us together in a tight brace
Doing the will of God in our lives is one of the keys to a good base.
So trust the lord and be patient, and in all your ways, try not to be in a haste
Because God gave you a talent, and you must not let it go to waste.

We go to our heavenly father and seek his face
And when we have problems, the arms of Jesus is the right place.
When we make mistakes, there is no better one than Jesus to embrace
And with all the power that Jesus has, Satan doesn't know how to handle the case.

There is no one that compares to him, his shoes no one else can lace
The closer we get to God, the more he shows us his amazing grace.
Let us be closer to Jesus for his coming, and this event we can almost taste.

11.20.21

Dale Leighton Campbell

Who Is Our Father?

Fathers – God gave them the ability to instruct and how to lead.
They are the head of the household, an example of a special breed.
Coming down through the ages, being a leader was in their seed.
We absorb all the instruction they give and on them we feed.
But how many times did we do what we wanted, not taking heed?
So, he comes to us with that look that says, "Children, take up your books and read."

He wants the best for us, that is why he is so stern.
And whatever we do in his sight, his trust we must earn.
Many times we misbehave, but that is how we learn.

He provides everything we need, food,
clothing, and a roof over our head.
And he is always telling us stories of the
old tales before we go to bed.
And the next day to test us, he asks, "do
you remember what was said?"
And he would always say "Children, to be
successful, you must study your daily
bread."

Sometimes if we are going somewhere, he
gives us dough.
He teaches us to be satisfied and said no
one we must owe.
As a family, we have been through
everything, the highs, and the lows.
Yet, throughout the ups and the downs,
my father remains a pro.
Because from God, my father learned
everything he knows.

If we want to be the best fathers that we can,

You must do what is right and hold on to God's unchanging hand.

As fathers, God will teach us in life, how to make a stand.

For sure, our fathers of fathers will make our feet be established on the land.

06.2021

Dale Leighton Campbell

The Nature Of The Seasons

When the spring comes, no one has to tell
the plants to start springing
It's natural even when you hear the birds
start singing.
Then you will see nature coming alive all
around
You will see and hear wildlife making all
sort of sounds.
And when it comes to an end, you'll know
that spring is gone when the summer heat
hits you in the face
It's just here for a short time so make sure
you don't put it to waste.
It arrives one day early at dawn, and
before you know it, it's gone
So make sure whatever activities are
happening you must make due
Because just before you look, fall appears
right on cue.

Dale Leighton Campbell

And then you regret that what you did in the summer was just a few
But at least what you planted, you can cook it together and make a stew.
From the best of everything we planted, now we reap
So, we gather it all together in one heap.
Just like nature would, preparing for the winter's haul
We all have to prepare, even the insects that crawl.
So whatever you do, try not to stall
Because when you look in the rear-view, you will see the winter's fall.
So when you hear the phone ringing, don't be surprised that winter is on the call to let you know that it is here
And whether you like it or not, you better prepare.
So don't make up all kinds of excuses, I don't care

Dale Leighton Campbell

Well Mr. Winter, we have spring summer and fall to back you up, so you better beware.

And when you put them all together, there is nothing that can compare

For now, all the sting of winter is gone, we have no fear

Now we see all the seasons of nature, loose in the atmosphere.

3.4.22

Dale Leighton Campbell

Will You Do What I Say?

Make sure serving the Lord and being
obedient to his word is our main intention
It's about time we give our hearts to Jesus,
we couldn't wait for his conversion.

Now praying, fasting, and studying the
word of God is good for our digestion
So be careful what we hear or see because
Satan will try to send us strong illusions.

But our Father will give us power to put
the devil under subjection
And when we pass throughout the storm
Jesus will hold us tight to show his
affection

But if we are looking to do things our way,
we will find out it's nothing substantial

And if the devil has you from here to there, God is the one who will give the right direction.

So if we feel we have done wrong, the holy ghost will tug at our hearts with conviction
Even though Satan brings all sorts of distraction.

The spirit of the Lord will try to get our attention
So we pray to get closer to God and for souls to get saved when we have convention

Because just now, all what we are seeing will be over when God puts the devil in extinction
Then everything will have its own place when God comes to the conclusion.

3.20.22

Dale Leighton Campbell

Keep At It, Don't Stop

We wish we would have studied hard in school and sealed it in a bag
Even though you look different in your face, on you they put a tag
So when we think life is looking good, all of a sudden, it catches a snag
If we only paid attention in school and listened to the teachers, even though they nagged
Now everything we hear will seem like an overwhelming pressure to make us sag
So we try to let everyone know our freedom of speech, but our mouths, still they try to gag
But don't be surprised when things start to go wrong when you begin to brag
For the time that we have to do our work, we must be specific and try not to lag

Dale Leighton Campbell

And all the good advice our elders gave us,
don't let it be a drag
And don't let anyone stop you from
pursuing your goals to make you put up a
white flag.

3.4.22

Dale Leighton Campbell

For Someone Special

Mothers are special in every way to us
They try to resolve everything without causing a fuss
Next to our father in heaven, we can depend on them for trust
Especially when it comes to serving the Almighty, it is a must.

We had a bad day at school, came home crying, looking for advice
She said "Just remember, whatever is happening, Jesus paid the price,
And if we trust him, he will work out everything to be nice."

Early in the morning, I went to her with my stomach feeling ill
Down on her knees she went looking in the cabinet for a pill

Then she looked up to God and cried out
because she is holy ghost filled.

So, wherever they are, we are in their
thoughts everyday
That's why I know that when God
fashioned her, it was with special clay.
This is why we have a momentous
occasion every year in the month of May

So in everything, we salute them in love,
with hugs and kisses
For this day we will make dinner, clean up,
and wash the dishes.

Although we owe you more for all the
things you have done
Spending time with you these years, I
learned a lot, and it was fun.

You have seen it all in every way, and you have passed the test
And you live by the old paths of our fathers with the crest on your chest.

So let us put everything together in one word; **Mother**, *you are the best.*

5.6.21

Dale Leighton Campbell

Open The Gift That You Got

To show his love for mankind God gave us a gift
He is here for one thing only and that is to give us a lift
To change our hearts from sin to righteousness, as he makes a shift.

Everyone is getting ready for Christmas for the wrong reasons, making a fuss
Instead of keeping our eyes on Jesus and how we can gain his trust
Christmas should be all about Jesus Christ, God's gift to us.

If we are looking for a gift at this time, it should be salvation.
It is written in the bible for us, in true clarification

And when we acknowledge him, we give our lives to Jesus for his dedication.

The love that he has, it's for everyone, small or great
He presents himself as our saviour when he lifts our weight
As a promise, he will always be on time, never late
For this encourages us as believers to keep the faith.

The season is to remember what God has done
That he gave the world his one and only begotten son
To accept him in our lives and prepare us for the race we must run
But if we reject the saviour at any time then our lives will be done.

Dale Leighton Campbell

This Christmas let us remember to give someone a bite to eat
And if possible, provide for them when they come in off the street.

And if you can, give them clothes to wear
And ensure they know that Jesus cares.

The Christmas season is not all about exchanging gifts with each other
If we don't share God's son with everyone, then why bother?
So let us accept him in our hearts because there won't be another.

When we are cozy in front of the fire this Christmas season
Just remember, in everything we do, that Jesus is the reason

Dale Leighton Campbell

To him we give our trust

And to live for Christ-is-a-must.

It's Christmas!

12.21.21

Dale Leighton Campbell

Don't Let It Get To The Grave

If we have any problems or disputes with our immediate family, loved ones, friends, or even our family in Christ, we should let our feelings be known before it's too late. Meaning, if something is on your mind, speak up before it's too late.

Whatever there is on our minds, now is the time to talk, because when we die, it cannot be fixed. Those things we have on our minds about our loved ones, we must resolve that issue or situation now. Don't put it off for later, there might not be a later, and the thing you have to say has died and gone in the wind.

When we were supposed to speak, we didn't, and now it's too late. We must speak up and let our intentions be known.

There is something I wanted to talk about, it was on my mind for a long time, but I kept it bottled up inside of me. When I was ready, it was too late; my loved one had passed on and I didn't get to tell them how I felt, I didn't get to settle the issue before they went into the grave.

The pain of that burden you feel when you didn't let your request be known, is a feeling you have to feel for the rest of your life.

So let us love one another, comfort one another, and when we have something on our minds, about anything, speak about it and let it be known, before it goes to the grave where nothing can be fixed.

Let us resolve it now and let our intentions be made known, so that our minds will be at peace with our family, loved ones, and friends, and most of all we will be at peace with God.

8.21

Dale Leighton Campbell

Restoration. Healing. Unity

We can see God speaking in his word,
trying to give us restoration
And the effort is made for us as a prayer in
the book of Lamentations.

But if we are puff up, God will not use us
unless we are humble
So let us look to God as a rock, even when
the devil tries to make us stumble
But if we continue in sin, without turning,
then our lives will crumble.

Let us put all our trust in Jesus, and not go
by our feelings
Because we don't want to entertain Satan,
especially the sins that he is dealing.
Sometimes when we pray, it seems it only
goes as far as the ceiling

Let us come together in unity and restoration will be there for our healing.

Sometimes the hardest thing to do when we are wrong, is to turn
How many times do we have to fall in the same trap before we learn?

As Children of the living God, we must come to him in sincerity
Then will he answer us from heaven and show us his purity
To restore us with healing, then we take it out to the community in unity.

And when God has done everything for us, we come to the realization
That when things are restored, God will put us back into circulation.

4.8.22

Notes

Dale Leighton Campbell

Dale Leighton Campbell

Dale Leighton Campbell

Dale Leighton Campbell

About the Author

When I was born, my great grandmother predicted that I would be a smart one. However, as I grew, my mother would end up having to send me to a special school in order for me to learn. I had good athletic abilities, but I was not strong in academic areas, so we came to Canada thinking that it would be a better place for me to learn.

However, it didn't help, but there was something deep within me that I didn't know about. I always thought that my athletic ability would take me places, but God had deeper plans.

He said, "*If you commit yourself to me fully, I will give you confidence to accomplish anything*." Now I know what my great grandmother saw in me; it was a deep spirituality. She saw what my friends and family couldn't see, and now God has brought it out in the form of writing, at this stage in my life.

I give God all the glory for having confidence in me and now I can walk with him confidently as he directs my path.

- Dale Leighton Campbell

Dale Leighton Campbell

Thank you for reading.

May you be blessed on your journey.

Manufactured by Amazon.ca
Bolton, ON